The
CHRISTOPHER ROBIN
Verse Book

*with decorations
and illustrations in full colour*

by E. H. SHEPARD

The
CHRISTOPHER
ROBIN
Verse Book

by A. A. MILNE

DEAN
in association with Methuen Children's Books

Also by A.A. Milne

THE COMPLETE WINNIE-THE-POOH
THE WORLD OF CHRISTOPHER ROBIN
THE POOH STORY BOOK

First published in Great Britain 1969
by Methuen & Co Ltd
Reprinted 4 times
This edition published in 1992 by Dean
in association with Methuen Children's Books
Michelin House, 81 Fulham Road, London SW3 6RB
Reprinted 1993 (twice) and 1994
Text by A.A. Milne and
line illustrations by E.H. Shepard
Copyright under the Berne Convention
Compilation and new illustrations copyright © 1967
by E.P. Dutton and Co Inc
Produced by Mandarin Offset Ltd

ISBN 0 603 55031 2

From *When We Were Very Young*: Buckingham Palace, Halfway Down, Lines and Squares,
The Three Foxes, Rice Pudding, Happiness, Disobedience, The King's Breakfast, Hoppity,
At the Zoo, Teddy Bear, Before Tea and Vespers.
From *Now We Are Six*: Us Two, The Friend, The Engineer, Furry Bear, The Little Black Hen,
Swing Song, Sneezles, Binker, Buttercup Days, Come Out With Me and In the Dark

CONTENTS

Buckingham Palace

They're changing guard at Buckingham Palace—
Christopher Robin went down with Alice.
Alice is marrying one of the guard.
"A soldier's life is terrible hard,"

                                    Says Alice.

They're changing guard at Buckingham Palace—
Christopher Robin went down with Alice.

6

We saw a guard in a sentry-box.
"One of the sergeants looks after their socks,"
                                    Says Alice.

They're changing guard at Buckingham Palace—
Christopher Robin went down with Alice.
We looked for the King, but he never came.
"Well, God take care of him, all the same,"
                                    Says Alice.

They're changing guard at Buckingham Palace—
Christopher Robin went down with Alice.
They've great big parties inside the grounds.
"I wouldn't be King for a hundred pounds,"
                              Says Alice.

They're changing guard at Buckingham Palace—
Christopher Robin went down with Alice.
A face looked out, but it wasn't the King's.
"He's much too busy a-signing things,"
                              Says Alice.

They're changing guard at Buckingham Palace—
Christopher Robin went down with Alice.
"Do you think the King knows all about *me*?"
"Sure to, dear, but it's time for tea,"
                              Says Alice.

Us Two

Wherever I am, there's always Pooh,
There's always Pooh and Me.
Whatever I do, he wants to do,
"Where are you going today?" says Pooh:
"Well, that's very odd 'cos I was too.
    Let's go together," says Pooh, says he.
"Let's go together," says Pooh.

"What's twice eleven?" I said to Pooh.
    ("Twice what?" said Pooh to Me.)
"I *think* it ought to be twenty-two."
"Just what I think myself," said Pooh.
"It wasn't an easy sum to do,
    But that's what it is," said Pooh, said he.
"That's what it is," said Pooh.

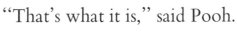

"Let's look for dragons," I said to Pooh.
"Yes, let's," said Pooh to Me.
  We crossed the river and found a few—
"Yes, those are dragons all right," said Pooh.
"As soon as I saw their beaks I knew.
  That's what they are," said Pooh, said he.
"That's what they are," said Pooh.

"Let's frighten the dragons," I said to Pooh.
"That's right," said Pooh to Me.
"*I'm* not afraid," I said to Pooh,
  And I held his paw and I shouted "Shoo!
  Silly old dragons!"—and off they flew.

"I wasn't afraid," said Pooh, said he,
"I'm *never* afraid with you."

So wherever I am, there's always Pooh,
There's always Pooh and Me.
"What would I do?" I said to Pooh,
"If it wasn't for you," and Pooh said: "True,
It isn't much fun for One, but Two
Can stick together," says Pooh, says he.
"That's how it is," says Pooh.

Halfway Down

Halfway down the stairs
Is a stair
Where I sit.
There isn't any
Other stair
Quite like
It.
I'm not at the bottom,
I'm not at the top;
So this is the stair
Where
I always
Stop.

Halfway up the stairs
Isn't up,
And isn't down.
It isn't in the nursery,
It isn't in the town.
And all sorts of funny thoughts
Run round my head:
"It isn't really
Anywhere!
It's somewhere else
Instead!"

Lines and Squares

Whenever I walk in a London street,
I'm ever so careful to watch my feet;
   And I keep in the squares,
   And the masses of bears,
Who wait at the corners all ready to eat
The sillies who tread on the lines of the street,
   Go back to their lairs,
   And I say to them, "Bears,
   Just look how I'm walking in all of the squares!"

And the little bears growl to each other, "He's mine,
As soon as he's silly and steps on a line."
And some of the bigger bears try to pretend
That they came round the corner to look for a friend;
And they try to pretend that nobody cares
Whether you walk on the lines or squares.
But only the sillies believe their talk;
It's ever so portant how you walk.
And it's ever so jolly to call out, "Bears,
Just watch me walking in all the squares!"

The Friend

There are lots and lots of people who are always asking
    things,
Like Dates and Pounds-and-ounces and the names of funny
    Kings,
And the answer's either Sixpence or A Hundred Inches
    Long,
And I know they'll think me silly if I get the answer wrong.

So Pooh and I go whispering, and Pooh looks very bright,
And says, "Well, *I* say sixpence, but I don't suppose I'm
    right."
And then it doesn't matter what the answer ought to be,
'Cos if he's right, I'm Right, and if he's wrong, it isn't Me.

The Three Foxes

Once upon a time there were three little foxes
Who didn't wear stockings, and they didn't wear sockses,
But they all had handkerchiefs to blow their noses,
And they kept their handkerchiefs in cardboard boxes.

They lived in the forest in three little houses,
And they didn't wear coats, and they didn't wear trousies.
They ran through the woods on their little bare tootsies,
And they played "Touch last" with a family of mouses.

They didn't go shopping in the
High Street shopses,
But caught what they wanted in
the woods and copses.
They all went fishing, and they
caught three wormses,
They went out hunting, and they
caught three wopses.

They went to a Fair, and they all won prizes—
Three plum-puddingses and three mince-pieses.
They rode on elephants and swang on swingses,
And hit three coco-nuts at coco-nut shieses.

That's all that I know of the three little foxes
Who kept their handkerchiefs in cardboard boxes.
They lived in the forest in three little houses,
But they didn't wear coats and they didn't wear trousies,
And they didn't wear stockings and they didn't wear sockses.

19

Rice Pudding

What is the matter with Mary Jane?
She's crying with all her might and main,
And she won't eat her dinner—rice pudding again—
What *is* the matter with Mary Jane?

What is the matter with Mary Jane?
I've promised her dolls and a daisy-
 chain,
And a book about animals—all in
 vain—
What *is* the matter with Mary Jane?

What is the matter with Mary Jane?
She's perfectly well, and she hasn't
    a pain;
But, look at her, now she's
    beginning again!—
What *is* the matter with Mary Jane?

What is the matter with Mary Jane?
I've promised her sweets and a ride
    in the train,
And I've begged her to stop for a
    bit and explain—
What *is* the matter with Mary Jane?

What is the matter with Mary Jane?
She's perfectly well and she hasn't
    a pain,
And it's lovely rice pudding for dinner
    again!—
What *is* the matter with Mary Jane?

Happiness

John had
Great Big
Waterproof
Boots on;
John had a
Great Big
Waterproof
Hat;
John had a
Great Big
Waterproof
Mackintosh—
And that
(Said John)
Is
That.

Disobedience

James James
Morrison Morrison
Weatherby George Dupree
Took great
Care of his Mother,
Though he was only three.
James James
Said to his Mother,
"Mother," he said, said he:
"You must never go down to the end of the town, if
   you don't go down with me."

James James
Morrison's Mother
Put on a golden gown,
James James
Morrison's Mother
Drove to the end of the town.
James James
Morrison's Mother
Said to herself, said she:
"I can get right down to the end of the town
   and be back in time
   for tea."

King John
Put up a notice,
"LOST or STOLEN or STRAYED!
JAMES JAMES
MORRISON'S MOTHER
SEEMS TO HAVE BEEN MISLAID.
LAST SEEN
WANDERING VAGUELY:
QUITE OF HER OWN ACCORD,
SHE TRIED TO GET DOWN TO
THE END OF THE TOWN—
FORTY SHILLINGS
REWARD!"

James James
Morrison Morrison
(Commonly known as Jim)
Told his
Other relations
Not to go blaming *him*.
James James
Said to his Mother,
"Mother," he said, said he:
"You must *never* go down to the end of the town without
    consulting me."

James James
Morrison's mother
Hasn't been heard of since.
King John
Said he was sorry,
So did the Queen and Prince.
King John
(Somebody told me)
Said to a man he knew:
"If people go down to the end of the town, well, what can
    anyone do?"

(*Now then, very softly*)

J. J.
M. M.
W. G. Du P.
Took great
C/o his M*****
Though he was only 3.
J. J.
Said to his M*****

"M*****," he said, said he:
"You–must–never–go–down–to–the–end–of–the–town–
    if–you–don't–go–down–with ME!"

The Engineer

Let it rain!
Who cares?
I've a train
Upstairs,
With a brake
Which I make
From a string
Sort of thing,
Which works
In jerks,
'Cos it drops
In the spring,
Which stops
With the string,

And the wheels
All stick
So quick
That it feels
Like a thing
That you make
With a brake,
Not string. . . .

So that's what I make,
When the day's all wet.
It's a good sort of brake
But it hasn't worked yet.

Furry Bear

If I were a bear,
   And a big bear too,
I shouldn't much care
   If it froze or snew;
I shouldn't much mind
   If it snowed or friz—
I'd be all fur-lined
   With a coat like his!

For I'd have fur boots and a brown fur wrap,
And brown fur knickers and a big fur cap.
I'd have a fur muffle-ruff to cover my jaws,
And brown fur mittens on my big brown paws.
With a big brown furry-down up to my head,
I'd sleep all the winter in a big fur bed.

The King's Breakfast

The King asked
The Queen, and
The Queen asked
The Dairymaid:
"Could we have some butter for
The Royal slice of bread?"
The Queen asked
The Dairymaid,
The Dairymaid
Said, "Certainly,
I'll go and tell
The cow
Now
Before she goes to bed."

The Dairymaid
She curtsied,
And went and told
The Alderney:
"Don't forget the butter for
The Royal slice of bread."

The Alderney
Said sleepily:
"You'd better tell
His Majesty
That many people nowadays
Like marmalade
Instead."

The Dairymaid
Said, "Fancy!"
And went to
Her Majesty.
She curtsied to the Queen, and
She turned a little red:
"Excuse me,
Your Majesty,

For taking of
The liberty,
But marmalade is tasty, if
It's very
Thickly
Spread."

The Queen said
"Oh!"
And went to
His Majesty:
"Talking of the butter for
The Royal slice of bread,
Many people
Think that
Marmalade
Is nicer.
Would you like to try a little
Marmalade
Instead?"

The King said,
"Bother!"
And then he said,
"Oh, deary me!"
The King sobbed, "Oh, deary me!"
And went back to bed.

"Nobody,"
He whimpered,
"Could call me
A fussy man;
I *only* want
A little bit
Of butter for
My bread!"

The Queen said,
"There, there!"
And went to
The Dairymaid.
The Dairymaid
Said, "There, there!"
And went to the shed.
The cow said,
"There, there!

I didn't really
Mean it;
Here's milk for his porringer
And butter for his bread."
The Queen took
The butter
And brought it to
His Majesty;

The King said,
"Butter, eh?"
And bounced out of bed.
"Nobody," he said,
As he kissed her
Tenderly,
"Nobody," he said,
As he slid down
The banisters,
"Nobody,
My darling,
Could call me
A fussy man—
BUT

I do like a little bit of butter to my bread!"

The Little Black Hen

Berryman and Baxter,
  Prettiboy and Penn
And old Farmer Middleton
  Are five big men . . .
And all of them were after
  The Little Black Hen.

She ran quickly,
  They ran fast;
Baxter was first, and
  Berryman was last.

34

I sat and watched
   By the old plum-tree . . .
She squawked through the hedge
   And she came to me.

The Little Black Hen
   Said, "Oh, it's you!"
I said, "Thank you,
   How do you do?
And please will you tell me,
   Little Black Hen,
What did they want,
   Those five big men?"

35

The Little Black Hen
　　She said to me:
"They want me to lay them
　　An egg for tea.
If they were Emperors,
　　If they were Kings,
I'm much too busy
　　To lay them things."

"I'm not a King
　　And I haven't a crown;
I climb up trees,
　　And I tumble down.
I can shut one eye,
　　I can count to ten,
So lay me an egg, please,
　　Little Black Hen."

The Little Black Hen said,
　"What will you pay,
If I lay you an egg
　　For Easter Day?"

"I'll give you a Please
　　And a How-do-you-do,
I'll show you the Bear
　　Who lives in the Zoo,

I'll show you the nettle-place
    On my leg,
If you'll lay me a great big
    Eastery egg."

The Little Black Hen
    Said, "I don't care
For a How-do-you-do
    Or a Big-brown-bear,
But I'll lay you a beautiful
    Eastery egg,
If you'll show me the nettle-place
    On your leg."

I showed her the place
    Where I had my sting.
She touched it gently
    With one black wing.
"Nettles don't hurt
    If you count to ten.
And now for the egg,"
    Said the Little Black Hen.

When I wake up
    On Easter Day,
I shall see my egg
    She's promised to lay.

37

If I were Emperors,
  If I were Kings,
It couldn't be fuller
  Of wonderful things.

Berryman and Baxter,
  Prettiboy and Penn,
And Old Farmer Middleton
  Are five big men.
All of them are wanting
  An egg for their tea,
But the Little Black Hen is much too busy,
The Little Black Hen is *much* too busy,
The Little Black Hen is MUCH too busy . . .
  She's laying my egg for me!

Swing Song

Here I go up in my swing
    Ever so high.
I am the King of the fields, and the King
    Of the town.
I am the King of the earth, and the King
    Of the sky.
Here I go up in my swing . . .
    Now I go down.

Sneezles

Christopher Robin
Had wheezles
And sneezles,
They bundled him
Into
His bed.
They gave him what goes
With a cold in the nose,
And some more for a cold
In the head.
They wondered
If wheezles
Could turn
Into measles,
If sneezles
Would turn
Into mumps;
They examined his chest
For a rash,
And the rest
Of his body for swellings and lumps.

They sent for some doctors
In sneezles

And wheezles
To tell them what ought
To be done.

All sorts and conditions
Of famous physicians
Came hurrying round
At a run.
They all made a note
Of the state of his throat,
They asked if he suffered from thirst;
They asked if the sneezles
Came *after* the wheezles,
Or if the first sneezle
Came first.
They said, "If you teazle
A sneezle
Or wheezle,
A measle
May easily grow.
But humour or pleazle
The wheezle
Or sneezle,
The measle
Will certainly go."

41

They expounded the reazles
For sneezles
And wheezles,
The manner of measles
When new.
They said, "If he freezles
In draughts and in breezles,
Then PHTHEEZLES
May even ensue."

Christopher Robin
Got up in the morning,
The sneezles had vanished away.
And the look in his eye
Seemed to say to the sky,
"Now, how to amuse them today?"

Binker

Binker—what I call him—is a secret of my own,
And Binker is the reason why I never feel alone.
Playing in the nursery, sitting on the stair,
Whatever I am busy at, Binker will be there.

    Oh, Daddy is clever, he's a clever sort of man,
    And Mummy is the best since the world began,
    And Nanny is Nanny, and I call her Nan—
            But they can't
            See
            Binker.

Binker's always talking, 'cos I'm teaching him to speak:
He sometimes likes to do it in a funny sort of squeak,
And he sometimes likes to do it in a hoodling sort of roar . . .
And I have to do it for him 'cos his throat is rather sore.

Oh, Daddy is clever, he's a clever sort of man,
And Mummy knows all that anybody can.
And Nanny is Nanny, and I call her Nan—
      But they don't
      Know
      Binker.

Binker's brave as lions when we're running in the park;
Binker's brave as tigers when we're lying in the dark;
Binker's brave as elephants. He never, never cries . . .
Except (like other people) when the soap gets in his eyes.

Oh, Daddy is Daddy, he's a Daddy sort of man,
And Mummy is as Mummy as anybody can,
And Nanny is Nanny, and I call her Nan . . .
 But they're not
 Like
 Binker.

Binker isn't greedy, but he does like things to eat,
So I have to say to people when they're giving me a sweet,
"Oh, Binker wants a chocolate, so could you give me two?"
And then I eat it for him, 'cos his teeth are rather new.

Well, I'm very fond of Daddy, but
 he hasn't time to play,
And I'm very fond of Mummy,
 but she sometimes goes
 away,
And I'm often cross with Nanny
 when she wants to brush
 my hair . . .
But Binker's always Binker, and is
 certain to be there.

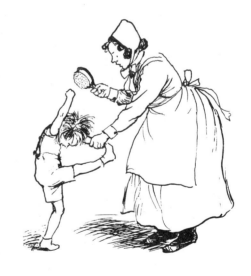

Hoppity

Christopher Robin goes
Hoppity, hoppity,
Hoppity, hoppity, hop.
Whenever I tell him
Politely to stop it, he
Says he can't possibly stop.

If he stopped hopping, he couldn't go anywhere,
Poor little Christopher
Couldn't go anywhere . . .
That's why he *always* goes
Hoppity, hoppity,
Hoppity,
Hoppity,
Hop.

At the Zoo

There are lions and roaring tigers, and enormous camels and
    things,
There are biffalo-buffalo-bisons, and a great big bear with
    wings,
There's a sort of a tiny potamus, and a tiny nosserus too—
But *I* gave buns to the elephant when *I* went down to the
    Zoo!

There are badgers and bidgers and bodgers, and a Super-
    intendent's House,

There are masses of goats, and a Polar, and different kinds
of mouse,
And I think there's a sort of a something which is called a
wallaboo—
But *I* gave buns to the elephant when *I* went down to the
Zoo!

If you try to talk to the bison, he never quite understands;
You can't shake hands with a mingo—he doesn't like shaking
hands.
And lions and roaring tigers hate saying, "How do you
do?"—
But *I* give buns to the elephant when *I* go down to the Zoo!

Buttercup Days

Where is Anne?
    Head above the buttercups,
Walking by the stream,
    Down among the buttercups.
Where is Anne?
Walking with her man,
Lost in a dream,
    Lost among the buttercups.

What has she got in that little brown head?
Wonderful thoughts which can never be said.
What has she got in that firm little fist of hers?
Somebody's thumb, and it feels like Christopher's.

Where is Anne?
Close to her man.
Brown head, gold head,
    In and out the buttercups.

49

Teddy Bear

A bear, however hard he tries,
Grows tubby without exercise.
Our Teddy Bear is short and fat
Which is not to be wondered at;
He gets what exercise he can
By falling off the ottoman,
But generally seems to lack
The energy to clamber back.

Now tubbiness is just the thing
Which gets a fellow wondering;
And Teddy worried lots about
The fact that he was rather stout.
He thought: "If only I were thin!
But how does anyone begin?"
He thought: "It really isn't fair
To grudge me exercise and air."

For many weeks he pressed in vain
His nose against the window-pane,
And envied those who walked about
Reducing their unwanted stout.
None of the people he could see
"Is quite" (he said) "as fat as me!"
Then, with a still more moving sigh,
"I mean" (he said) "as fat as I!"

Now Teddy, as was only right,
Slept in the ottoman at night,
And with him crowded in as well
More animals than I can tell;
Not only these, but books and things,
Such as a kind relation brings—
Old tales of "Once upon a time,"
And history retold in rhyme.

One night it happened that he took
A peep at an old picture-book,
Wherein he came across by chance
The picture of a King of France
(A stoutish man) and, down below,
These words: "King Louis So and So,
Nicknamed 'The Handsome!'" There he sat,
And (think of it!) the man was fat!

Our bear rejoiced like anything
To read about this famous King,
Nicknamed "The Handsome." There he sat,
And certainly the man was fat.
Nicknamed "The Handsome." Not a doubt
The man was definitely stout.
Why then, a bear (for all his tub)
Might yet be named "The Handsome Cub!"

"Might yet be named." Or did he mean
That years ago he "might have been"?
For now he felt a slight misgiving:
"Is Louis So and So still living?
Fashions in beauty have a way
Of altering from day to day.
Is 'Handsome Louis' with us yet?
Unfortunately I forget."

Next morning (nose to window-pane)
The doubt occurred to him again.
One question hammered in his head:
"Is he alive or is he dead?"
Thus, nose to pane, he pondered; but
The lattice window, loosely shut,
Swung open. With one startled "Oh!"
Our Teddy disappeared below.

There happened to be passing by
A plump man with a twinkling eye,
Who, seeing Teddy in the street,
Raised him politely to his feet,
And murmured kindly in his ear
Soft words of comfort and of cheer:
"Well, well!" "Allow me!" "Not at all."
"Tut-tut! A very nasty fall."

Our Teddy answered not a word;
It's doubtful if he even heard.
Our bear could only look and look:
The stout man in the picture-book!
That "handsome" King—could this be he,
This man of adiposity?
"Impossible," he thought. "But still,
No harm in asking. Yes I will!"

"Are you," he said, "by any chance
His Majesty the King of France?"
The other answered, "I am that,"
Bowed stiffly, and removed his hat;
Then said, "Excuse me," with an air,
"But is it Mr. Edward Bear?"
And Teddy, bending very low,
Replied politely, "Even so!"

53

They stood beneath the window there,
The King and Mr. Edward Bear,
And, handsome, if a trifle fat,
Talked carelessly of this and that . . .
Then said His Majesty, "Well, well,
I must get on," and rang the bell.
"Your bear, I think," he smiled. "Good-day!"
And turned, and went upon his way.

A bear, however hard he tries,
Grows tubby without exercise.
Our Teddy Bear is short and fat,
Which is not to be wondered at.
But do you think it worries him
To know that he is far from slim?
No, just the other way about—
He's *proud* of being short and stout.

Come Out with Me

There's sun on the river and sun on the hill . . .
You can hear the sea if you stand quite still!
There's eight new puppies at Roundabout Farm—
And I saw an old sailor with only one arm!

But every one says, "Run along!"
(Run along, run along!)
All of them say, "Run along! I'm busy as can be."
Every one says, "Run along,
There's a little darling!"
If I'm a little darling, why don't they run with me?

There's wind on the river and wind on the hill . . .
There's a dark dead water-wheel under the mill!
I saw a fly which had just been drowned—
And I know where a rabbit goes into the ground!

But every one says, "Run along!"
(Run along, run along!)
All of them say, "Yes, dear," and never notice me.
Every one says, "Run along,
There's a little darling!"
If I'm a little darling, why won't they come and see?

Before Tea

Emmeline
Has not been seen
For more than a week.
　　She slipped between
The two tall trees at the
　　end of the green . . .
We all went after her. *"Emmeline!"*

"Emmeline,
　I didn't mean—
　I only said that your hands weren't clean."
We went to the trees at the end of the green . . .
But Emmeline
Was not to be seen.

Emmeline
Came slipping between
The two tall trees at the
　　end of the green.
We all ran up to her. "Emmeline!
Where have you been?
Where have you been?
Why, it's more than a week!" And Emmeline
Said, "Sillies, I went and saw the Queen.
She says my hands are *purfickly* clean!"

In the Dark

I've had my supper,
  And *had* my supper,
    And *HAD* my supper and all;
I've heard the story
  Of Cinderella,
    And how she went to the ball;
I've cleaned my teeth,
  And I've said my prayers,
    And I've cleaned and said them right;
And they've all of them been
  And kissed me lots,
    They've all of them said "Good-night."

So—here I am in the dark alone,
  There's nobody here to see;

    I think to myself,
    I play to myself,
  And nobody knows what I say to myself;
Here I am in the dark alone,
  What is it going to be?
I can think whatever I like to think,
I can play whatever I like to play,
I can laugh whatever I like to laugh,
  There's nobody here but me.

I'm talking to a rabbit . . .
  I'm talking to the sun . . .

I think I am a hundred—
    I'm one.
I'm lying in a forest . . .
    I'm lying in a cave . . .
I'm talking to a Dragon . . .
    I'm BRAVE.
I'm lying on my left side . . .
    I'm lying on my right . . .
I'll play a lot tomorrow . . .

   .   .   .   .

I'll think a lot tomorrow . . .

   .   .   .   .

I'll laugh . . .

            a lot . . .

               tomorrow . . .
            (*Heigh-ho!*)
                 Good-night.

Vespers

Little Boy kneels at the foot of the bed,
Droops on the little hands little gold head.
Hush! Hush! Whisper who dares!
Christopher Robin is saying his prayers.

God bless Mummy. I know that's right.
Wasn't it fun in the bath tonight?
The cold's so cold, and the hot's so hot.
Oh! *God bless Daddy*—I quite forgot.

If I open my fingers a little bit more,
I can see Nanny's dressing-gown on the door.
It's a beautiful blue, but it hasn't a hood.
Oh! *God bless Nanny and make her good.*

Mine has a hood, and I lie in bed,
And pull the hood right over my head,
And I shut my eyes, and I curl up small,
And nobody knows that I'm there at all.

Oh! *Thank you, God, for a lovely day.*
And what was the other I had to say?
I said "Bless Daddy," so what can it be?
Oh! Now I remember. *God bless Me.*

Little Boy kneels at the foot of the bed,
Droops on the little hands little gold head.
Hush! Hush! Whisper who dares!
Christopher Robin is saying his prayers.

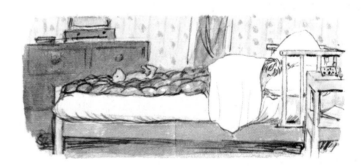